Praise for *Little Things Long Remembered*

"*Little Things…* promises—and delivers—a treasure chest of ideas to build cherished memories and strong family connections. Keep this book close by." –Judy Blume

"Newman's tips for making grand family memories are so easy to implement that every parent will want to grab a few to try right away. Integral to each 'little thing' is the warmth and love we want our kids to take away with them from their too-swiftly-over growing up years." –Susan K. Perry, PhD, author of *Playing Smart*, *Kylie's Heel*, and a blogger for *Psychology Today*

"Skip the elaborate birthday party with a petting zoo or laser tag. If you really want to show your kids that you love them, read *Little Things Long Remembered*. Susan Newman lists lots of little things that make your kids feel special every day of the year." –Jen Singer, author of *You're a Good Mom (and Your Kids Aren't So Bad Either)*

"Here's a book that gets it: We may not have time to create elaborate meals or do-it-yourself projects, but we want our kids to look back on a childhood sparkling with memories, including some imperfect ones. If you need a nudge to help you start creating them, this is the book for you—nudge, nudge." –Lenore Skenazy, author of the book and blog *Free-Range Kids*

"For today's busy parents, this is a treasure trove of ways to engage children, build close family bonds, and ensure special memories for years to come." –Marilyn Price-Mitchell, PhD, developmental psychologist and founder, National ParentNet Association

"*Little Things Long Remembered* is full of simple ideas for making ordinary days (and holidays we grown-ups sometimes rush through) fun, surprising, and memorable for children. Parents often worry how to prepare children for an uncertain future, but Susan Newman reminds us that it's the present—and the bond we build with our kids each day—that really matters." –Carlin Flora, journalist and author of *Friendfluence: The Surprising Ways Friends Makes Us Who We Are*

"This wonderful book warms parents' hearts and offers them timeless, easy-to-deliver, valuable advice for building a loving connection with their children." –Jeffrey Bernstein, PhD, author of *10 Days to a Less Defiant Child*

"Psychologist Susan Newman once again showcases her creativity and keen eye for family life in *Little Things Long Remembered*. She reminds us that trust is best forged in small, everyday exchanges with children. Here is a wealth of simple, doable ideas—some barely a sentence long—for bettering adult/child relationships, one special moment at a time. This is a book anyone who spends time with a child will want to keep handy." –Melinda Blau, author (with the late Tracy Hogg) of *Family Whispering: The Baby Whisperer's Commonsense Strategies for Communicating and Connecting with the People You Love and Making Your Whole Family Stronger*

Little Things
Long Remembered

Making Your Children Feel Special Every Day

Susan Newman, PhD

A previous edition of this book was published by
Random House/Crown.

Little Things Long Remembered
Copyright © 1993, 2014 Susan Newman, PhD
New Edition published by
Iron Gate Press

Publisher's Cataloging-In-Publication Data
(Prepared by The Donohue Group, Inc.)

Newman, Susan.
  Little things long remembered: making your children feel special every day /
Susan Newman, PhD. -- New edition.

   pages : illustrations ; cm

  First edition: New York: Crown Publishers, c1993.
  "500+ sure-fire, stellar ways"--Cover.
  Issued also as an ebook.
  ISBN: 978-0-9914660-0-9

  1. Parenting--Miscellanea. 2. Child rearing--Miscellanea. 3. Parent and child--
Miscellanea. I. Title.

HQ755.8 .N53 2014
649/.1

Editorial Production: Janet Spencer King, www.bookdevelopmentgroup.com
Cover/Interior Design: LMW Design Studio, www.lmwdesign.com

This book may be purchased for groups or promotional use. Contact the author via her
website: www.susannewmanphd.com

Printed in the United States of America for Worldwide Distribution
ISBN: 978-0-9914660-0-9
ISBN e-book: 978-0-9914660-1-6

Other Books by Susan Newman

The Case for the Only Child: Your Essential Guide

Under One Roof Again:
All Grown Up and (Re)learning to Live Together Happily

The Book of NO: 250 Ways to Say It—and Mean It and
Stop People-Pleasing Forever

Nobody's Baby Now: Reinventing Your Adult Relationship
with Your Mother and Father

Parenting an Only Child: The Joys and Challenges of
Raising Your One and Only

Little Things Long Remembered:
Making Your Children Feel Special Every Day *(First Edition)*

Little Things Mean a Lot: Creating Happy Memories
with Your Grandchildren

Little Things Shared: Lasting Connections Between
Family & Friends

Getting Your Child into College: What Parents Must Know

Let's Always ... Promises to Make Love Last

Don't Be S.A.D.:
A Teenage Guide to Stress, Anxiety & Depression

It Won't Happen to Me:
True Stories of Teen Alcohol and Drug Abuse

You Can Say No to a Drink or a Drug:
What Every Kid Should Know

Never Say Yes to a Stranger:
What Your Child Must Know to Stay Safe

Memorable Birthdays: Now a Guide, Later a Gift

To all the children and parents

who shared their

meaningful and special

"little things" with me.

CONTENTS

Introduction

Two decades ago I wrote the original version of *Little Things Long Remembered.* Its intent was to be a treasure-trove of ideas for parents to create special ties to and long-lasting memories with their children. Memories are, after all, a precious gift.

The book sold ... and sold at a steady pace for nearly 20 years! With so many changes in society and technology taking place during those years, it became clear to me that it was now time to update the book. The intent of this new edition remains the same: to be a collection of reference points for parents that enable them to create a backlog of heartwarming memories with their children and have fun while doing so. Whether you are a stay-at-home or a working parent, the suggestions in these pages will help keep you connected to your children and will contribute to building a strong, loving family.

I started gathering ideas when my stepchildren and my son were very young. Over the years I discovered hundreds of ideas that, when enacted for the long haul, added much more to family life than memories. My children, now adults, send me pictures of the sunflowers they grow that become even taller than those we grew as a family project. The holiday traditions we celebrated have become part of my grandchildren's lives as well. This continuing of our family's "little things" is reassuring to all of us and is a critical factor in what keeps us close and makes us all smile.

Life swirls at a hectic pace in most families today. That reality places a high premium on finding family time. *Little Things Long Remembered* is designed to help maximize whatever time you have together— be it a minute or two, five minutes, a weekend, or a holiday. Small parcels of time well used assure stellar memories—and ultimately, memories and traditions are the backbone of family unity...and the glue that holds family together.

With the click of a mouse, technology provides a whole array of ways to create and save what you and your children do; thus, memories need never be lost. Consider this book your personal think-tank for being a standout parent and a takeoff point that will spark your own ideas. The time you spend with your children and what you choose to embrace from within these pages will become as memorable and meaningful to *you* as they will be to them.

Connecting

Whether your child is a toddler or teen, there is a great deal of fun to be had. Starting traditions and making memories is much easier than you may think.

Admittedly, it is a challenge to keep up with your own *and* your children's activities and commitments. When you sometimes feel you are out of touch with your children, look through *Little Things Long Remembered.* You will find ways to bring you and your children closer while making efficient use of everyone's available but generally scarce time. It is possible to stay involved no matter how busy you are. This book is your guide for feeding your children's memory banks.

You cannot and will not want to do everything mentioned, and you will probably need to adjust some of the "little things" as your children get older. But you will be amazed at how many "connections" you can make with a child in a single day. The rituals and traditions, even the gestures, add to children's sense of security, teach them values, and shore up their identities—all priceless, far beyond the joy of any individual "little thing."

Realize that children's reactions are unpredictable. You never know which gesture, tradition, or offbeat, spur-of-the-moment adventure or misadventure will become a "little thing long remembered," embedded happily in their minds forever.

Children are unique memory keepers. Siblings often recall situations and events differently, and some may not remember them at all. Furthermore, what you think of as an important event, your children may forget all about. The goal, then, is not to worry about achieving perfection but to enjoy what you decide to do.

The Cardinal Rules

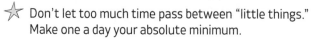

★ Don't let too much time pass between "little things." Make one a day your absolute minimum.

★ When time is short, deliver a hug, a kiss, and a daily, "I love you."

★ Give up some social commitments to carve out more time to spend with your children.

★ At home, focus as much as possible on your kids. Put away electronic devices so you can really "be" with them.

★ Save some energy during your busy day to enjoy your sons and daughters.

★ Don't decrease discipline because you feel guilty about the time you spend at work or away from your children.

★ Choose activities you like; children can tell when you are not having fun and are "faking it."

★ Forget attempts to make picture-perfect memories. Often the mistakes or the unexpected things are what kids remember best. Mishaps can be hilarious and make loving family memories for all.

★ Repeat, repeat. Repetition creates tradition and is the key to happy memories of growing up ... and to glowing memories of you.

★ Remember, the most precious time is the time spent with your children.

Establishing Ties

When the rat race takes over, it's understandable to forget the obvious. Here's a list with an abundance of essential gestures—many familiar but possibly forgotten, others new and untried in your family—to keep you connected to your offspring. Pick and choose to match your needs and your children's ages and personalities.

It is never too late to start a routine that makes everyone feel wanted and happy. Your attention will make your children feel good about themselves, and their delighted responses will be your big reward. You can give the following ideas your all with surprisingly little effort.

A Special Place

Keep an extra chair or stool in the kitchen, den, or next to your desk or workshop area so your child can be with you to watch, talk, or help.

Hello-Goodbye

Be sure you always give and receive hello and goodbye kisses from your children. If you don't get them, ask. Turn coming-and-going kisses and hugs into must-do rituals. Make it fun by asking, "Did you forget something?" when someone starts to leave without the indispensable kiss or hug.

House Rule

If there's been a misunderstanding or disagreement between you and your child or between your child and a sibling, address it before bedtime. Figure out what went wrong and how it might be resolved.

Early Start

Kiss your kids goodbye even if they're asleep when you leave.

Hi, Kids, I'm Home

Whenever you arrive home from work, try to be cheerful and happy to see your children no matter how exhausting and stressful your day has been.

Role Model

Explaining how *you* spent your day encourages a child to open up and pour out the details of his day.

Designer Kiss

Develop a kiss that is unique to your family—your trademark. Maybe it's two pecks on the tip of the nose, one peck on each cheek, or one long, two short kisses on the forehead.

Special Delivery

Create a gesture that your child knows means "I love you." Perhaps it's your hand on your heart, your arms folded, or placing one finger on your cheek. Use it often and when your child least expects it—at a school event or sports game, in the grocery store, or when out with friends or relatives.

"I Want to Hold Your Hand"

The Beatles had the right idea when they wrote that song. Whatever happened to hand-holding? Bring it back long after you would routinely hold your child's hand as a safety precaution. But do keep in mind that at different stages, children balk at a parent's public affection. Respect their wishes.

Silent Communication

A thumbs up, both hands out to the sides, some quiet clapping, the peace sign, a wink, or a gentle tug on an ear lobe—try any one of these as a silent symbol of your family's camaraderie to be used by both parents and children.

Compliments

Compliment your child *and* let your child overhear you bragging about her to someone else.

Show Off

Use a photo your child has taken as your screensaver or wallpaper on your computer and other devices … or ask him for help in choosing the image to display.

It's My Mom's

Lend your daughter a piece of your costume jewelry to wear to school or on the weekend.

It's My Dad's

Lend your daughter a tie—an old one—to wear as a belt. Lend your son a tie—one he likes—to wear as a tie.

Establishing Ties

How Pretty
Wear whatever "jewels" your child makes or buys for you.

I Chose You
Tell your child how much you enjoy being his parent. Children like to hear that they are loved and fun to be with.

On the Day You Were Born
What happened? Your child wants to know the time and circumstances around her birth. Who saw me first? Who came to visit? Did I cry a lot? Tell her story often, spotting it with some funny things that may have happened before and after she was born.

Garbage Detail
Involve your child in some decisions about chores, particularly who does what and when. Children are generally more receptive and helpful when they have a say in what they are asked or required to do.

King of the Tissue Box

Put one child in charge of keeping toilet paper under the bathroom sink, another for keeping the paper towel holder filled, and still another for making sure there are always tissue boxes in the appropriate rooms. Small offbeat tasks make big memories, particularly when a "title" is tagged to them.

Bravo

Let your child know that you are happy with his successes, be they great or modest. Don't compare him with his friends or siblings.

Important Hugs

One-on-one hugs tell a child she is special. When you embrace your child, give her and the hug your full attention.

Believer

For as long as your child believes, do your job as the tooth fairy.

Sorry

Admit when you're wrong.

Establishing Ties

Penalty Box

Allow your children to have some input into their own punishments. Ask them to come up with penalties for acting up, ignoring your requests, or lying. They are more likely to behave when they have had a say in the consequences. Someday they may even think back and decide they were too hard on themselves in the penalties they chose.

Pet Names

Come up with an affectionate and endearing nickname that your child likes—Petunia, Pumpkin, or Rocket. As your child gets older, don't drop the pet name, but use it wisely to avoid embarrassment now or later.

Mom, Come Look

If it's important enough for your child to ask you to see something he has done, it's important enough for you to take a look.

You are Valued

Praise the effort that went into a job well done and say thank you for tasks your child completes, be they for you or for her.

Be All Ears

"You're not listening," is generally a parent's cry to a child. Don't make that mistake yourself. To understand what is going on in her life, stop what you are doing, turn around, and look her in the eye when she is telling you something.

Kids Play Cop

Decide how many times a day you will say no or nag your children. Turn refusals and nagging into a game of sorts by telling your children the number and giving them permission to remind you when you are getting close to using up your daily allotment.

Be in a Yes Mood

Agree or give in to a request when your children least expect it. A sprinkling of yeses goes a long way in adding to kids' contentment and sense of their parents as fair.

I Want It Too

Consult your child when it's time to buy birthday gifts for his friends. You'll also find out what your child would like when he tells you what he thinks is a good present for a friend.

Establishing Ties

Clearing the Air

When you're upset by something that happened during your day and are ranting and raving about it at home, be sure to let your child know that you are not angry with her. Considering your child's feelings helps bridge the gap between office and home emotions.

Not Now

Children are not responsible for the number of hours you work. Don't use "I'm tired" as an excuse too often.

I'm Proud

Every day ask your child what she did that day that she is proud of. Helped a friend? Did well in a game? Received a good grade? Brushed the dog?

Leave On the Light

What may seem silly to adults matters to children. Respect their wishes to leave on the hall light or to not tell someone something they feel is humiliating.

Lights Out!

Make it a competitive game to turn out the lights when you leave a room. Try to catch Mom or Dad, sister or brother when they forget, and consider a "punishment," perhaps an extra chore.

You Can Always Reach Me
Talk to your children about how to reach you and make sure they know how to do so.

That's Great!
Get excited when your child tells you about his day or an upcoming event. Nodding your head is not enough.

Quick Peek
Slip a picture of you or the family into your child's pocket or backpack.

Food, Glorious Food
Yes, the way to a child's heart is often through her stomach. Pick out one of her favorite snacks when you are zipping down the supermarket aisles.

What's Mine is Yours
Dive into a hot fudge sundae together. Share an apple or a banana. Split a piece of pie for dessert.

Dinner Bell
Have a "chain call" to bring everyone to the table: Pam calls Lisa, Lisa calls Beth, and Beth calls Pete. Or ring a bell to call the family together.

Establishing Ties

Musical Chairs

Once in a while or on a specific day each week, rotate seating positions at the kitchen or dining room table so children each have a turn at the head of the table.

Double Desserts

Once a month or whenever you happen to have extra, shock your children by announcing double-dessert night.

★ ★ ★ ★

Kid Fix

Request a "kid fix" (a hefty hug and big kiss) whenever you feel the need, and let your child know it makes you feel better.

Kissing Monster

Be impossibly affectionate: call yourself the "kissing monster" and plant kisses on your child in rapid profusion. Delight and laughter will abound.

Not the Teacher's Pet

During rough periods at school, be understanding. Don't be quick to jump on the teacher's bandwagon. Hear your child's point of view too.

Lumpy Vases and Paper Flowers

If your child made it, find a special place for it—not in a bottom drawer or on a closet shelf. Take his "bowl" to the office to hold paper clips or put it on a counter for holding keys, scissors or eyeglasses. Put fake flowers in her leaky "vase."

Share the Seasons

Point out glorious leaf colors in the fall and a snow-capped mountain in the winter. There's a joy in introducing your child to, and sharing the natural beauty of, the ever-changing seasons—or one unusual sight in the landscape.

Also Known As

Always put the flowers, a.k.a. weeds, that your child picks for you in water.

What a Fine Family This Is!

Flaunt your pride in the family by placing framed family photographs on tables and walls around the house. Put a group photo in your child's room where she can easily see it.

Establishing Ties

Shoe Store

Designate a handy chair or step near the door for tying shoelaces, securing Velcro closures, or pulling on boots. Call it the "shoe store" and invite your children in. This will speed up getting ready and they will remember it as going to the "shoe store."

Diner

"Nothing could be finer than to eat in mother's diner." Label your kitchen counter the "diner" and sing the refrain when you serve up short-order meals or snacks.

Study Hall

Use the same table, couch, or chair for reviewing material for a test.

How's Ricky?

Inquire about your children's friends regularly.

Caring Questions

How was your spelling test? History test? Did you win the game? Was the Book Fair fun? If you know something important was on the schedule that day, remember to ask about it.

Reduce Kid Overload

Eliminate or cut back some of your children's activities so your free time is not spent shuttling or waiting for them. Let them weigh-in on what they would like to reduce or eliminate. This will leave them more time for making memories.

Good Secrets Only

Parent and child can giggle about the secret, enjoy the suspense, and be proud of each other for keeping the secret so long. Good secrets only: what's for dinner, a gift for another member of the family, holiday plans, or a surprise visitor.

Ties that Bind

Inform your children when relatives send their love or leave a special message. Keep children up-to-date on family news.

From Our House to Yours

Create a family web page with your child's input and send the link to relatives and close friends. Be sure to keep it current. You might want to put older children in charge of adding news.

Establishing Ties

Once a Day

Tell your children you love them at least once a day—when you send your kids off to school, when you tuck them in at night, or anytime in between. More is always better in this instance.

Architect's Delight

Ask for your child's ideas on any home renovation plans, especially if they include her bedroom.

Young Decorator

When sprucing up your child's room, allow him to decide what color (paint, sheets, curtains) or theme he prefers. Give choices if you do not want to offer limitless options (such as white or beige walls, or this wallpaper design or that).

Museum Quality

Your kids will feel proud if you frame one or more of their paintings. Find places around the house—hallways, stairwells, or bathrooms—to hang or display your children's best "work" (clay dinosaur, wooden box, drawing … and more).

Go Ahead, Try It

Encourage your child to try new things—to enter a contest, request information, write a song, or build a snowman—then praise that effort.

The Driving Passion

Be interested in what interests your child, not in what you want or hope her passion will be. This allows you to be together more often, talking about and exploring *her* passion.

Be Sympathetic

Don't dismiss a child's problems lightly. Pay attention to what has happened and take the time to hear your child out. Offer concerned, thoughtful advice. You can do that in a minute or two.

Five Minutes More or Less

Given what is on everyone's calendars, you may think you are too busy to squeeze in meaningful exchanges. You are not. Five minutes talking about acts of kindness, singing a family song, or shooting baskets solidifies the parent-child bond. In between the fast-paced lives you and your children lead, you can stay connected with little things that mean a lot to children. They will remember even short, impromptu activities as well as your longer, affirming interactions.

May I Have This Dance?

After dinner turn on some music and dance with your children for a few minutes.

Action Central

Keep a bulletin board, whiteboard, large pad, or notebook centrally located—in the kitchen, at the bottom of the stairs, or near the back door—where everyone can leave notes or messages for each other. Perhaps, "Off to my friend Melissa's house." Or, "I love you. XOXO, Mom."

Share a Calendar

Enter the family birthdays, activities, performances, and meetings on one electronic calendar. Refer to it together when arranging the day's or week's schedule. A computerized or paper calendar keeps everyone in the family up-to-date and feeling included.

Ciao, Bonjour, Buenos Días

Learn how to say hello or thank you in different languages, or take five minutes every day to learn different words in the same language. Progress to learning how to speak the language your children seem most interested in or are learning in school. Borrow a language CD from the library or order one online for help.

Two Sugars

Ask your child to join you for a "cup" of coffee or tea. Dilute with milk and add a touch of sugar, according to age.

Getting to Know You

Do you know your child's favorite color? Favorite television show? Favorite cartoon character? Favorite game? Book? Sport? When you know her preferences you know her better. Share yours.

Five Minutes More or Less

Review
Go over—or in the least glance at—your child's school papers as often as you can. Ask to see them if your child doesn't offer them to you.

Photosynthesis
Discuss what your child is studying, be it fossils, math problems, or photosynthesis.

Good Morning
Initiate a wake-up routine: several kisses, a stuffed animal search, two hugs, a double alarm, or sending the dog to jump on your child's bed.

Bugle Call
Be creative. Make up a wake-up song to sing each morning that includes your children's names.

You've Got Mail
When early departures and late meetings have you missing your child, send a text message, e-mail or musical e-greeting as a sweet reminder that you love her.

Continuous Story

Start a story: "A boy named Jack had a fun family." Alternate one-sentence additions: one child adds the next sentence and another child continues the story. And so it goes for the car ride, at the dinner table, or while waiting anywhere.

Acts of Kindness

Ask your children to share one kind, caring thing they did each day...or plan to do tomorrow.

Mom or Dad: "At the store, I helped a lady carry her packages to the car."

Child One: "I shared my cupcake with Sean."

Child Two: "I will let my sister go first tomorrow."

A Word or Fact a Day

There are apps galore giving anything from a sports or science fact a day to a new word a day. Find apps for your gadgets online and make choices that coincide with your children's ages and interests.

Pretzels, Please

Prepare the grocery list together—at the dinner table or on a special pad kept on the kitchen counter.

Five Minutes More or Less

Soup or Salad

Include your children in meal planning. Children have surprisingly good suggestions—if it's only to tell you the soup, vegetable, or dessert they prefer—and are more likely to eat what they asked for.

Mix It Up

Make an Italian or Mexican meal one night, Chinese or Indian another.

You Name It

Meatless Mondays, Fishy Fridays, or Kid-Choice Wednesdays. Naming the meal day tells children what is for dinner and becomes a unique part of growing up in your family.

For No Reason

When the whole family is together, give each member a similar token surprise. Call it an "S" to heighten the fun. It could be a pair of socks, a flower, a set of stickers, a pad, a pen, a box of crayons, or a book. The suspense of not knowing when there will be an "S" is what makes this a little thing long remembered.

Stockbrokers in the Making

Choose a stock for each member of the family or for the whole family to follow. It's exciting for children to see a stock's progress and to feel part of your grown-up world. You do not have to purchase a stock to make tracking one interesting and instructive, but the one you choose should relate in some way to your children's lives: perhaps a food company that makes their favorite snack or a tech company that makes their game device.

Ha, Ha!

Tell your child jokes and laugh at his.

Zooming In

Whenever you are taking pictures or video, hand over the camera. Ask your youngster to take some shots. Using an adult's camera, whether on your cellphone, iPad, or other gadget, is serious business to a young child, and the pictures are a reminder of that special privilege.

Photo Gallery

Print and hang snapshots of special family times—canoeing with a cousin, biking with parents, or feeding baby sister—on a mirror or bulletin board in the kitchen, family room or in your child's room. Replace dated photos with new ones.

Five Minutes More or Less

Sing a Song of 25 Cents
Make up words to go with popular children's songs and nursery rhymes. Original lyrics can be hilarious, whether set to "Row, Row, Row Your Boat" or to your own tunes.

I Like It Too
At home and in the car, listen to your child's favorite songs and sing along with her. Join in with a strong voice for the catchy verses and refrains.

We are the Smiths
Create a song that includes the names of favorite family members. Sing it regularly, incorporating the names of new cousins, aunts, or uncles as well.

Where You Stand
Express your opinions. By doing so you share your values and beliefs and let your child know what you think.

The Waiting Game
Count players on the field, babies in the doctor's waiting room, pictures on the wall, cars you pass, red objects, green objects, or people in line in front of you. Call it "the waiting game." Playing it will make the time go faster.

Not Fair
Encourage your children to bring complaints about each other or an unfair rule to a "round table" for a family discussion. Be open to compromise or suggestions that will rectify the situation.

You're Doing Fine
Share your thoughts about school and the teacher with your child when you return from an open house or any meetings you have with the teachers. Your enthusiasm counts.

Accentuate the Positive
Go overboard when praising a good report card or school project. Read the teacher's comments with or to your child and emphasize his hard work and diligence.

Saved
Saving schoolwork shows you're interested and encourages a child to do better. Mark on a cardboard or plastic box, "Allison: 2nd Grade." During the year drop in papers that you wish to save or all the papers to be sorted at a later date.

Keeping Company

Ask your child to keep you company when you fold laundry or wrap presents, when you write notes or are just relaxing. Ask him just to be there with you.

Act Silly

Chase your child through the house, pretend to be an airplane and soar down on her, or do something out of the ordinary and utterly ridiculous. Be out-and-out silly.

Switching Roles

As an occasional surprise, complete one of your child's regular chores: feed the dog, set the table, or make her bed.

In an Emergency

Go over home safety rules and emergency procedures including dialing 911. Establish which neighbors your children can go to in an emergency, and take steps to make the kids comfortable with them.

Best/Worst

On a regular basis, ask your kids what was the best and worst part of their day or week.

Did You Practice?

Five minutes of your undivided attention while your child practices his musical instrument is more encouraging than 500 pleas to practice.

Duets

Sing while she plays, or play while she sings or dances. Joint performances demonstrate your support and can be hilarious.

Applause, Applause

Never be too busy to watch your children's impromptu magic or puppet shows and plays. Watch willingly; clap loudly.

So Big

Mark and date an out-of-the-way wall periodically with your kids' growth patterns. Use different color pencils for each child.

Spades, Hearts, Diamonds, and Clubs

Teach your child a card trick or card game.

My Allowance, Please

Discuss what your child plans to save for or spend his allowance on.

Five Minutes More or Less

Precious Extra Time Together
Schedule and floor space permitting, exercise in your child's bedroom while she dresses for school.

Just Say No
Ask your child to picture himself saying no to alcohol and other drugs. Have him practice his stand with you.

Lush Plants
Grow a plant together. Stick toothpicks in a sweet potato, put the potato in a glass of water, and check it every few days. Or try growing an avocado seed or grapefruit pits. Plenty of instruction online.

It's a Sign
Scribble a sign on a shirt cardboard or large piece of paper to encourage, support, or praise your child. Write "GO" as support for an upcoming competition or "CONGRATULATIONS" for an honor received or completion of a large project. It's a sure sign that you care.

Whiter than White
Brush your teeth with the kids in the morning. It's more fun for young children to have company while they do what they consider a tiresome chore.

Closer than Close

Lather up your child's face and give him or her a razor *without* a blade to shave alongside you. Splash on a few drops of cologne.

Lunch Box Messages

Napkins are a great place for humorous drawings, short notes, or messages of love. How many children actually use their napkins anyway?

The Everything Sandwich

This combination sandwich, too fat for ordinary mouths, is piled high with a little bit of everything your child loves. Serve it on a weekend.

Checking In

Touch base with your child in the middle of the day or right after school to share her latest excitement, which may long be forgotten by the time you get home.

Goodnight Call

Call in your goodnight kiss and promise an in-person one as soon as you come home.

Just Rewards

Treat your child to an ice cream or frozen yogurt, a cookie, or a doughnut after a visit to the doctor or dentist.

Noted: I Love You

Leave notes in your child's room, in a schoolbook, or on the kitchen counter for him to find.

At the Library

When you are in the library or bookstore picking out books for yourself, stop in the children's section and select a few books for your kids.

With Love

Inscribe all books you give your children with loving messages and the date.

Little Things from Other Places

Bring home chopsticks or fortune cookies from a Chinese lunch, or bring a few mints or a packet of sugar (for a child to use on her morning cereal) from a restaurant dinner.

Catching ... Up

Every now and then, spend five minutes before dinner tossing a baseball or football. Mark a calendar with a ball or a check mark to keep track of how well you're catching up.

Thank You

Send your child a blank card filled in with a message of appreciation: "Thank you for helping me rake the leaves," or, "Thanks for cleaning up your room," or, "Thank you for helping out with your baby brother."

Mail Call

Hold the mail until the entire family is home. Open it together. Give young children the advertisements, catalogs, and bulk mail that you don't read.

Dear Jamie

Send your child a quick note or letter once a week or once a month that tells about what he's been doing or the fun he's been having. Save the letters on your computer if that is where you write them.

Last Licks

Call the kids to lick the beaters and the bowl whenever you bake.

Share Your Computer

Open a file in your computer for your child. Together create documents for whatever she wishes: her birthday guest lists, Christmas wish lists, letters to a pen pal, or book reports. These files will be revisited many times over by you for sure, and by your son or daughter too.

Puzzle Mania

Before or after dinner each evening, work on assembling an age-appropriate jigsaw puzzle together. Keep it on an out-of-the-way table or a tray so you can move it if you need the space.

Bull's-Eye

Hang a dartboard in an out-of-the-way corner, ready for a round of target practice when you have a few minutes to spare.

Note: Suction-cup dart games are safe for young children.

How Was Your Day?

Go around the dinner table and have everyone—that means parents too—tell something about their day. Let each person talk as long as he or she would like.

Personalized Stories
Tailor a story around your child—how she learned to put her head underwater, wash her own hair, climb the stairs, reach the refrigerator door, play a new game, or dress herself. The story can be chock-full of friends she played with or places she went.

I Vote for the Grand Canyon
Call a family meeting during dinner to discuss vacation plans. Explain options. Let children express their feelings about one choice versus another.

Curious George
When dinner conversation goes flat, retitle your children's favorite books and ask them to explain how they think the new story line would work. For example, Curious George Moves In With (insert your child's favorite TV personality or movie star). Do this with any popular titles and current celebrities to create lots of laughs.

Newsmakers
Discuss a current event nightly or once a week. Select topics of interest to children: record-breaking sales for a toy, an outstanding athletic performance, a medical discovery, or an ecological advance.

Five Minutes More or Less

What Should I Wear?
Ask your child to help you select your clothing for the next day (limit the choices to two).

Observe
Sit back, relax, and enjoy watching your child involved in an activity. He or she knows you are watching and to a child that is particularly important.

Snack Time
If you're not going to be home for the evening, schedule a snack break with your child before you leave or when you return home.

Feeling Very Special
Reserve a different plate or cup for snack time use only. This can be a plate or cup you used as a child or one your child received as a gift from a favorite relative. Decorated paper plates and cups also separate snack time from regular meals and make snack time an anticipated event.

Crazy Spelling
When helping your child study for spelling tests, tie each word on the list into a fantasy story about him, the family, or an upcoming trip or occasion.

I Give!

An abbreviated wrestling match provides physical contact. For the less aggressive, try tickling. And if you don't care for rolling around on the floor, substitute arm wrestling.

Room Visiting

Make a practice of reading a book or the newspaper in your child's room while she is playing, reading, or getting ready for bed.

Things Grown-Ups Don't Do

Start a gentle pillow fight with your child.

Sports Fanatics

Discuss yesterday's ballgames, matches, and players' stats with your child.

Tub-Side

While you have a captive audience, use this time to sing songs and play with younger children or to talk with older children who still want company.

Five Minutes More or Less

Chit-Chats
Spend a few minutes on the end of your child's bed or in a cozy armchair talking. Keep conversations light and non-critical. As chit-chats become routine, you or your child can comfortably request one when there is something important to discuss.

Once More
When your child discovers a book she loves, read it again and again if so requested.

Reading Rituals
Remember, older children like to be read to long after they can read themselves. Share one chapter a night.

Mark My Place
Use or create a unique bookmark with your child to hold your place after nightly reading.

What's Happening?
Show an interest in what your children are reading by asking them to summarize the plot for you every now and then—but not for every book. Anything mandatory is no longer fun.

We're All in Our Places

A nightly routine of putting away or arranging key stuffed animals under the covers alerts your child that it is almost time to go to sleep. If named, call stuffed animals by name before a last "goodnight" to your child.

Remember When?

Children adore stories about a parent's childhood, especially incidents in which you were embarrassed or did something "stupid."

When You Were Young

Youngsters delight in hearing about their own "youth." Five-year-olds love to be told what they did that was smart or funny when they were two or three years old. Tell them about their first words, words they couldn't quite pronounce, and the funny ways they crawled or climbed.

Grandma's Version

Ask grandparents to tell your children stories about raising you and about your childhood.

Five Minutes More or Less

Draw or Scribble
Requesting a picture to send or give to Grandma makes a child feel important. Ask for a picture for Daddy's or Mommy's office. And one for Aunt Debra … you get the idea.

You Tell Me
Have the children create their own bedtime stories.

Complaint Headquarters
Call yourself the "Complaint Department" and "be open" before final tuck-in so your child can get what, if anything, is bothering him off his chest.

Lullaby and Goodnight
Sing the same song or lullaby with your child each night.

I'm Too Old
Sing your child nursery rhymes and lullabies long after they seem appropriate. Your child will tell you she's too old for "that one," but love that you keep doing it.

Vanishing Monsters

A colorful spray bottle filled with water will help make any "lurking monsters" disappear from the bedroom. Have your child spray wherever he thinks the monsters live—under his bed, in the closet, or by the window.

Blankie–for Reading Only

Keep a special blanket or throw to be used exclusively for telling bedtime stories and reading books while snuggled together.

Nightly Fanfare

Have a quick bedtime ceremony even if it's only a certain way of puffing the pillow or patting your child's head. Fly a blanket in the air in the elaborate style of a magician before it lands on the bed; tuck the top sheet a special way.

Fanfare Continued

In your absence have the baby sitter follow your nighttime rituals as closely as possible.

Five Minutes More or Less

Nice Note
At bedtime have your child tell you something good that happened that day. It's a positive note to go to sleep on.

Not Home Stories
When you know that you will not be home at bedtime, either record your story for the baby sitter to play or arrange to Skype to read to your child from wherever you are.

Anticipation
Talk about plans for the upcoming weekend. Get your child's input.

Suggestion Box
Ask your children to write down what they would like to do again or what would be new to your family. Keep suggestions in a basket or box and pull one out when, in fact, you have more time to spend together.

Half an Hour to an Hour or So

The years a child prefers to spend time with his parents speed by. If you don't connect now, relating when he or she is older will be more difficult. Take advantage of all opportunities. Virtually everything you do together brings you closer and has the potential to become a fond memory—even cleaning the fish tank, washing the windows or the car, or swinging in a hammock on Sunday afternoons. Right now you have no way to judge what will turn into a happy time when your child rethinks his or her childhood.

Smooth Start

Eat breakfast with your child. You'll have time to be sure he has his lunch money, books, sneakers, and other necessities for his day. If you're together for breakfast he might not mind your occasional absence at dinner.

I'm Early

Arrive home a half an hour or so earlier than usual to play in the yard or nearby park before dark with your child.

Sand Castles

Climb in the sandbox. Dig and build too.

Escort

Every now and then, go into the office late so that you can take your child to school, even if it's only once a month or once every few months.

At Your Level

Get on the floor and spend time pretending to cook in the play kitchen or to deliver goods with the toy trucks. Help build a skyscraper with blocks or a fort with empty boxes. The more time on the floor, the longer you will be remembered for playing with your son or daughter.

In the Game

Jump rope with the children even if you are not sure you can still do it. Being able to laugh at Mom's or Dad's stumbles is the point.

Boxed

Hopscotch is a perennial favorite. Join in or teach
your child how, then play.

Get with the Program

Okay, "Teach," show me how. Have your child teach
you how to use a new computer program, calling
her "Teach" the entire time. Create website IDs and
passwords together.

Mountain Climbing in ...

Choose a landmark or country that interests your
child and spend time exploring it via search engines
and websites. When interest wanes, look up another
place you and your family are not likely to visit.

Take Me Out to the Ballgame

Go to see a minor or major league team if there is one
close by. And be sure to have someone take a picture
of all of you in your seats.

In a Long Line

Start a family tree using an online genealogy site.
Begin by including as much as you know. You or the
children can ask older relatives for more information
and leads. With new leads, you will be ready to dig for
more information.

Early Risers
Watch a sunrise (or sunset) together.

Getting to Know You
Early in the school year, take time to meet all of your child's teachers and coaches, and even the bus driver. This way if you have to call, you will have relevant names and associations when you are discussing your child.

Back-to-School
Leave a short note in your child's desk or notebook no matter how old she is that tells her how much you enjoyed visiting her classroom and meeting her teacher on back-to-school night.

You're Getting Me That!
When your child least expects it, take him to the store and buy something he's been longing to own.

You Were So Adorable
Go through your photo albums, whether they are in picture books or stored online, and describe what your children were doing when the pictures were taken. Show your own childhood pictures and talk about what you did "way back then."

Picture This

Ask your child to help you select the photos to go into the family album—be it paper or digital. Computer savvy kids will want to make their own online albums. Ask your son or daughter to organize your digital or scanned photographs to create a family album and title it, "Album by Jordan."

Mani-Pedi/Rose Red

Whether polishing nails at home or in a salon, every now and then, before a celebration, give your daughter a manicure and pedicure at the same time you do yours.

Feels Like a New Room

Many children like to rearrange the furniture in their rooms. Listen to their suggestions and offer to help move the bed or desk to the other wall if asked. Bring home something to brighten up the new arrangement.

Homebound Solos

Strengthen a child's sense of individuality with time alone with you at least once a week—talking, reading, cooking, or playing a game—without involving a brother or sister. Create simple "alone time" coupons good for different amounts of time—an hour, 15 minutes, the whole afternoon—for children to return to you as they are used.

Beauty Shop

Give your daughter a new hairstyle one evening— a French braid, a few curls, a ponytail tied in one of your hair clips or holders.

To the Gym

Create your own workout space at home with used equipment purchased inexpensively at yard or garage sales. Your child can join in according to her age and ability.

Up, Down, Side, Step

Although your child may not be able to keep up with you, invite him to join your home exercise program.

Car Wash

A car wash is a wonderfully messy job from a young child's point of view. You can always go over the streaky sections to finish the job.

Assistant to the Chef

You'll see more of your child if you enlist his services to fill the bread basket, carry dishes to the table, fill the salt and pepper shakers, or wash the lettuce.

Sup, Sup, Supper-Time

Be sure your family eats together unrushed as often as possible during the week—with television and electronic devices turned off.

Kids Cook

Have the children find a recipe, prepare the shopping list, and shop with you for the ingredients. You either supervise or, if they are old enough, sit nearby and read a book. They will be pleased with themselves when they, not you, put dinner on the table.

Tuesday is Lindsay's Night

Assign each member of the family a night that they are "responsible" for dinner. Everybody pitches in with the preparation. Even a four-year-old can help open packages or pour chocolate sauce over ice cream.

Candlelit Dinner

Once every few weeks put fresh flowers on the table, light dinner candles, and take a moment to express gratitude that you are a family.

Breakfast for Dinner

Unusual enough to be remembered and especially easy when time is short. Serve a dinner of waffles, pancakes, French toast, or other typically morning dishes—perhaps scrambled eggs and English muffins.

Junk Food Jaunt

Every now and then abandon the kitchen and surprise your child with dinner at her favorite spot.

What's Cooking?

Cook something with your child at least once a month. Quick recipes and prepared mixes work just fine to build this memory of cooking together.

Chef-in-Training

Invest in a children's cookbook to make food prep more interesting for your young chefs who will likely save their cookbook for decades to come.

Family Favorites

Start saving your children's favorite recipes on recipe cards or in the computer to give them access when it's time to help decide what's for dinner. Down the road, turn them into a cookbook for the kids to take with them when they go off on their own.

Half an Hour to an Hour or So

Lower Your Standards

There's a time and a place for takeout, delivery, or prepared foods. The point is togetherness, not gourmet dining every night.

Pizza Party

Try buying just the dough from your local pizza parlor, or look in the supermarket for another type of prepared crust. Bring it home and show the kids how to punch down and pull the dough into shape. Spread their favorite toppings and bake.

On Your Schedule

Bake a batch of cookies for your child's class. Store in your freezer until the time is right to send them in with a message: "Dear Class: Because you studied so hard for the health test," or, "Because you finished your science projects." *Not* because it's your child's birthday.

When You're Going Out

If you have evening plans, sit with your children while they eat dinner.

If You Must Do Work

When you have office work to do at home, invite your child to join you in "pretend office," using her coloring books or class assignments as her work.

Cast Your Ballot

Take your child to the polls with you when you vote.

Walkin 'n Talkin

Go for a brisk family stroll after dinner for exercise and to chat.

Twerpie Power

Definition: Imaginary extra strength children magically get anytime a parent needs help with a job. Call for "twerpie power" when you want something retrieved from upstairs, wood for the fire, or the dinner table set. The name somehow overrides the fact that you've asked for help.

Give Me a Break

In the middle of a chore or extended homework stint, offer a rest period complete with an unexpected cookie or frozen yogurt.

Half an Hour to an Hour or So

Car Talk

Use chauffeuring time wisely: talk with your child instead of listening to the radio (unless you are singing together).

Unplugged

Tuning out allows you to tune in to your children and they to you. Turn off cellphones, iPads, TVs, and other devices to give you undivided time together. It might be for only 15 minutes or half an hour, but why not try for an entire day on a weekend? Family time is more fulfilling without the constant interruption and interference of technology, and you will be amazed by what you hear. Make being unplugged a regular part of your family life.

Life After "Go Fish"

As children mature, card games such as I doubt it, crazy eights, hearts, casino, rummy, or gin can become family rituals. Determine what will be the winning score or set a time limit before you begin— or carry the game over to the next night or weekend when you all have a chance to pick up where you left off.

Game Time

When time is short, quick games satisfy, especially if you play them often. Checkers, tic-tac-toe, hangman, Backgammon, Uno, or a few rounds of Boggle do the trick.

Tournament of Tournaments

Select a game—Monopoly, Clue, Scrabble, or ping pong—and play it regularly, keeping an ongoing score. Leave board games set up for the next round. Card games are also excellent for tournament play.

Foul Shots

Shoot baskets in the local park, schoolyard, or in your own driveway.

Relax

You don't always have to be doing something with your children. Just being home and in the same room is often enough.

Joint Collections

Baseball cards, stamps, coins, board games, bottles, seashells, dollhouse furniture, calendars, or salt and pepper shakers—choose items you can all enjoy collecting and scout them out together on vacation or weekends.

Showtime

Do whatever it takes to be in the audience for your child's school plays, concerts, and other performances. He'll be looking for you.

Make a Production

Bring flowers to your "star," or take her out to lunch or dinner to make every performance a grand event. Take pictures in costume and post them on the refrigerator, kitchen bulletin board, and of course, on Facebook. Frame the best ones and display in a high-traffic area.

Van Gogh in the Making

Even if your art skills are non-existent, sketch or color with your child when asked. Amazing conversations and insights come across the calm of the drawing board.

Selective Volunteering

To keep in tune with your child's school life, volunteer at a weekend school fair or carnival booth.

Another Year Well Done

Celebrate the last day of the school year with a family lunch or dinner in a fancier restaurant than you would normally take the children. Dress up and make it an occasion.

Family Night

Three or four times each year, reserve one night for skits, charades, board games, or other activities that all family members can participate in no matter what their ages.

Batteries Charged

Don't neglect yourself. Tell your children that you are the "Energizer Bunny" and you need to recharge your batteries. Take a half an hour every now and then for self-time so you can have more fun with your kids.

Weekend Fun

Without plans, the family's weekends can slip into drudgery, filled with chores and errands or pure inertia. The extra effort it takes to plan activities together brings a family closer and makes being one of its younger members more exciting. The suggestions that follow range from universal to highly specialized. Select ones that suit you and your family's preferences and are appropriate for your children's ages. Set aside the hour or two you need on Saturday or Sunday to do a special activity with the kids. Whatever your choice, it will boost everyone's spirits and encourage closeness.

Over Easy with a Side of Bacon
Go out for breakfast or brunch on a Sunday morning.

Read the Comics ...
... to them until they can read them to you.

Oven Fresh
Doughnuts, bagels, or muffins warm from the bakery are a treat the whole family can anticipate. Take the children with you; let them help make the selections.

Pancake Skills

Shape breakfast pancakes into your child's initials. Or perhaps cook "silver dollars" or roly-poly flapjack people.

With a Twist

Include pretzel making as part of your family fare. Find a simple recipe online and twist away.

Be Prepared

Keep the house well-stocked with board games for rainy days and evenings. Playing with Mom or Dad is always a treat.

Artist's Corner

Too cold or too wet to go out? Have supplies at the ready in what will become known as the artist's nook. Store pipe cleaners, sequins, yarn, paper, clay, crayons, fabric pieces, and glue for your child to create whatever she imagines: puppets, flowers, animals, or costumes.

We Can Do it Now

Learn a new sport together. Take up cross-country skiing, aerobics, or hiking as a family. This may require some child prodding at first.

Weekend Fun

It's a Blue Jay

Study butterflies, birds, or plant life in your own backyard. Buy related books, borrow them from the library, or do online searches to investigate and explain what you discover or see.

Starry, Starry Skies

On a warm, clear evening, take blankets outside and look at the stars. Point out constellations and be prepared to explain what's behind their often strange names.

Firefighter

Visit the local fire station with your child.

S'il vous plaît ... Merci

Go to an ethnic restaurant and study up ahead of time to order in that particular language. It will be a living experience for the children to see that those funny foreign words you have been learning have real meaning and use.

Do-si-do

Attend a square dance as a family.

Up, Up, and Away

Try your hand at kite flying. Lots of laughs are likely when you can't get the kite in the air. Let your young children try too. Once you've made a successful launch, turn the "controls" over to your child.

Chop, Chop

That doesn't always mean hurry up. Preparing a taco dinner gives everyone a task. Younger children can mash an avocado while older children can help chop different vegetables and lettuce.

Highest Bidder

Investigate online auction sites to find original versions of games and toys you played with as a child. Your offspring will have something to say when they compare their updated games to yours.

Needed and Appreciated

Prepare a large pan of lasagna or a pot of stew with the kids for them to have for dinner. Reserve and deliver some of the delicious results to a housebound friend or sick relative.

Weekend Fun

Dog Walkers

If you don't have a dog in your family, you can ask the local dog shelter if it needs dog walkers. Volunteer for the job—it's good exercise for the dogs, for you, and for the children.

Down the River

Is there a river near you that has the right flow for tubing? Check local listings to find places that rent large tubes if you don't have access to your own. Take note of age and size restrictions for children.

Destination Ride

Orchestrate a family bicycle ride with an enticing reward in the middle or at the end—lunch, a swim, a double-dip ice cream cone, or a visit with someone special. To get your bearings of the area, pick up a map at a state park or scope out your route on the computer before you embark.

Flying High

Attend the local fair and take a ride that soars high with the kids. They will take pride in their scary adventure ... and remember the first time they rode amusement park rides with you.

Just a Little Bit Farther

Encourage your young swimmer to go with you
for a distance she believes may be too far for her.
Stay close; it's not a race and safety is paramount.
The smile on her face when she meets the goal
will be worth all your urging and encouragement.

Roasted Marshmallows

Start a fire in the fireplace and roast marshmallows.
During the summer, you can roast them over an
outdoor fire or grill.

Fireside Special

The perfect memory maker is a s'more: a roasted
marshmallow and sections of chocolate bars
sandwiched between two graham crackers. S'mores
are especially good on cold weekend evenings when
the family is sitting in front of the fire.

Cupcakes in the Making

Discover how the filling gets in the middle, how soda
gets its fizz, or how ice cream gets its flavors. Find
a food factory, bakery, or bottling company in your
area that gives tours. The manufacturing process with
its giant equipment, automation, and assembly lines
leaves a lasting impression.

Weekend Fun

Swinging

Set up a hammock between two trees and share lazy, restful moments in it together.

No Green Thumb Required

Plant tomatoes—cherry tomatoes do well—in a large clay pot or tub to set out on your deck or front porch. Put the children in charge of watering the plants and picking the tomatoes as they ripen.

Green Thumb Required

Start a garden with your children, even if you have only a small space. Plant vegetables they like and that grow quickly and in abundance—green beans, peas, tomatoes, zucchini, or cucumbers.

So Big

Sunflower plants grow as high as eight, ten, or more feet. Standing among the tall stalks and giant blooms will be something the kids will never forget.

So Fat

If you have the space, grow pumpkins from giant pumpkin seeds. These special seeds produce pumpkins that, once full-grown, can weigh 450 pounds or double that. Fortunately, growing normal-size pumpkins or watermelons is also a remarkable experience for children.

On the Beach
Build very large sand castles with moats and roads. Cars, snakes, and turtles are easy shapes to mold with moist sand.

Shell Seekers
To keep the spirit of a trip alive, designate the size, type, or shape—whether heart-shaped, arrowhead, or perfectly round—of seashells, rocks, and driftwood to find and put on a shelf when you return home.

Beginner Botany
Spend a day at the nearest botanical gardens. Check the schedule online for special festivals or children's activities. Many gardens have spring festival days in particular that are ideal for family picnics.

Major League Fun
Attend a spring training game for a major league baseball team. It is easier to catch foul balls and even score some autographs than during regular season games.

Minor League, Major Fun
Attend games of your local community's semi-professional sports teams.

Weekend Fun

All Wet
Put on your bathing suit and dash through the sprinklers with your children.

A Place of Their Own
Build a tree house or help your children build a fort—a special place to call their own that they will talk about for decades to come.

Super Sundaes
Arrange all the fixings—sprinkles, syrups, and fresh fruits—on the kitchen counter or picnic table. Let family members smother their own bowl of ice cream just the way they like it.

Bananas, Strawberries, Peaches
Try your hand at making ice cream using the fruit of the season. Search online for recipes that don't require an ice cream maker.

Foam and Fizz
Serve ice cream in a glass and let each person add his own cream soda or ginger ale to create an ice cream float that foams and fizzes.

The Capital is ...
Go to your state capital for the day or the weekend and learn about the local history.

Tide's Out
When the tide's out and the sandbar is in view, comb the sandbar and beach for sand dollars. Boil them with bleach to a milky white. When dry, they make prize mementos for the kids.

Rain, Rain, Go Away
Everyone gear up for a walk in the rain. Singing and jumping in the puddles, splashing permitted, is the memorable part.

After the Storm
Decide on an after-storm activity outside, perhaps to hunt for salamanders or bright-colored leaves.
Or in winter, shovel snow, go sledding, or make snow angels.

Muffin Mania
At the end of a fruit's peak growing season, make it a tradition to bake muffins with it.

Weekend Fun

Fall In

Form parent-child teams (or Mom and child vs. Dad)
to see who can rake the biggest pile of leaves together
for the children to jump or fall into.

Red, Yellow, Brown, and Orange

Go for a walk through the woods or around town
to collect the prettiest fall leaves to bring home. Put
them in a vase on the dining room or kitchen table.

Matinee Today

For a child, the chance to sit proudly next to Mom or
Dad in a darkened movie theater compensates well for
your long workweek at the office.

Monthly Movie

Select movies that appeal to the whole family to go to
or rent and watch at home. Invite the children to help
choose the movie.

Down, Boy!

Train or groom your dog together.

Hometown Times

If geographically feasible, take your kids on an excursion to the town of your childhood. Point out the movie theater, the basketball court or dance studio, and your elementary school—whatever structures from your childhood are still standing. Knock on the door of the house you grew up in to see if the current occupants will show your children through the house.

On Foot

Take a walking tour of your city or town. Look online for a map that guides you and points out surprising places of interest in the town where you live.

Tents and All

Be it a one-shot or a frequent activity, camping out offers opportunity for rich memories. At the very least you can pitch a tent in your own backyard.

For a Good Cause

Whether you're stuffing envelops for a fundraiser, pounding signs into the ground for a political campaign, or dropping off leaflets about your favorite cause, a child volunteer can be as helpful—and certainly as enthusiastic—as his parent.

Weekend Fun

Good Luck

Hunt for four-leaf clovers. Press the ones you find in a book that you are pretty sure will be around years from now.

Personal Best

With the help of technology, create a walking or jogging loop that starts and ends at your front door and that matches your youngster's age and ability. Pace your run or walk so that your child can keep up.

Personal Trainer

If you are easy going enough about jogging, let your child "pace" you on his bicycle. Assume going in that most of the time he'll be way ahead and doubling back.

Ferris Wheels and Roller Coasters

Attend the same fair or carnival every year.

The More the Merrier

Invite other families to eat and play games in your own backyard. Ask everyone to bring a dish; all you really need to supply is the game equipment.

Grilled with Frills

Have a cookout for your children's friends. Grill burgers or hot dogs and include kid-friendly frills: potato chips, popcorn, and pretzels.

The Oldies

Teach your children how to play marbles, jacks, or pick-up sticks. They might see why you liked these games so much.

Over the River and …

You and the kids gather together food for a picnic or meal at grandma's or another relative's home and go on a visit.

Change of Pace

Party food on paper plates by the fireplace constitutes a fine mid-winter indoor picnic.

Sloppy, Gooey, Slime

Slime is easy to clean up, easy to make, and endlessly fun in one or several colors. Look online for recipes. Search: "How to make slime."

Regulars

Have extended family members, grandparents, an aunt, an uncle, or cousins join you regularly at a family meal during the weekend.

Weekend Fun

Culinary Discoveries
Scan the Internet for new recipes and prepare them together as routine part of family life.

Family Night Reserved
Reserve one weekend evening for the family to stay home and do something together—play games or cook together or tackle a long ignored project.

Surprise Guest
Invite a surprise person—an old family friend, a relative, or one of your child's friends—to dinner and keep it a secret until he or she walks in the door.

Dad's Night Out
Every now and then, maybe once a month, select a night for just Dad and the children to do something fun. Go a bit heavy on the special treats.

Mom's Night Out
Same as above: just Mom and the kids.

Dress Up
While you're dressing for an evening out, your child can don clothing you no longer wear. Save it in a box or bag on the floor of your closet for these occasions.

Never Know What You'll Find
Spend a few hours scouting flea markets or garage sales. Given a minimal amount of money, a child can unearth what he believes is a treasure—which it may well be one day.

Family Doubles
Pair up for tennis as soon as your children show an interest in the game. They will enjoy being on the court even if they can't hit the ball over the net. In a few years family tennis will be fun for parents too.

Museum Piece
Working in short stretches of time, if that's all you have, put together a model airplane, boat, or car with your child. No matter how it turns out, displayed on a shelf, the "masterpiece" will be laughed at or admired for years to come.

Pickings Not Slim
Schedule an afternoon of strawberry, blueberry, raspberry, or apple picking. Local harvest dates and locations are listed in newspapers and on the Internet.

More Whipped Cream, Please
Serve strawberry or blueberry shortcake with what you picked.

Jam Session
Children can help the adults gather and prepare the fruit in season, add the necessary ingredients, and stir the pot. Failed (runny) jam is a delicious replacement for chocolate syrup.

The Art of Homemade
Someday your children are going to want you to pass along recipes. The ones they'll ask for are most apt to be those you are teaching them today to make or bake, the ones that are definite favorites. First step: Ask them to help.

Bumper Bowling
With the gutters blocked, knocking down some pins is a no-miss proposition for the youngest bowlers. Call or check online to find where and when local alleys offer bumper bowling.

The Big Bite
Drop a fishing line from a bridge or cast it from the edge of a creek. Many municipalities stock their lakes, ponds, and streams with fish, and sporting goods stores often rent poles. Check to see if you need a fishing permit, and find out the best lure and bait for catching local fish. Bring your cellphone or camera to take pictures of the catch.

In the Ocean
When the tide is low, search for crabs or scallops. Dig for clams. Wear water shoes or old sneakers.

In the Trees
In the fall, go on a hunt for abandoned birds' nests.

Back-Seat Parent
Car trips are enjoyable excursions if you can keep children occupied. Be the ever-prepared parent by packing hand-held games, age-appropriate travel toys, a small pillow, and a blanket for each young child. Wherever you go, the car ride itself may become the memory.

Imagine If
What would you do if you were mayor of your city? Principal of your school? Owner of a baseball team? Conductor of an orchestra? Ask the children for their ideas as you drive to your destination or during dinner.

Ms. Fix-It
Teach your daughters and sons how to use a hammer and screwdriver.

Chores that Bond

Certain jobs, when tackled as a team, can be fun and breed a warm brand of togetherness: raking leaves, planting a garden, and straightening out the toy chest. The jobs children complain about the loudest are sometimes the ones they most often recall with fondness.

Permanent Structures

When making lasting changes to your property—creating a walkway, adding shrubs, building a fence, or breaking ground for a garden—have your child work with you. Years later, the project will become the tree she planted or the fence he built.

Fisher & Company

Have your son or daughter join you to fix a pipe, trim the shrubs, or wash the windows. Your child's sense of accomplishment is enhanced when you joke about the fact that it was "another job well done by Fisher (your family name) & Co."

Party Time

Make a big deal out of shopping for important-occasion attire for your children to wear.

Just Like Mom's/Dad's

When shopping for special family events such as weddings or Christmas dinner, buy an accessory that (almost) matches Mom's or a shirt or jacket that resembles Dad's.

Annual Shopping Spree

Focus attention on your child by making a day of back-to-school shopping even if she needs only shoes and a notebook. Go to lunch afterwards.

Please Touch

Choose a hands-on museum or children's museum over a regular museum if you have a choice. Interactive museums are stimulating and more enjoyable for the young set.

Victory

Celebrate your "pro" team by wearing the team colors when watching the game. Hold a victory celebration when the team wins (this could just be loud cheering as a group in front of the television set).

The Perfect Excuse

Use Derby Day or Super Bowl Sunday as an excuse to invite friends and their children over to watch the event and to share sandwiches or pizza.

Major Decisions
Have the children help plan an evening—including where to eat and what to do after dinner.

Very Noisy
Visit the pet store. It's fun to look, although quite tempting.

Super Hero
Buy the longest Italian bread you can find and lots of sandwich fixings. Let each person add a layer, then cut your bulging super hero into sections. Or, divide the bread first and have each person prepare his own.

The Collector
Help your young collector—of stamps, coins, baseball cards, or comic books—by attending a special show, getting books on the subject out of the library, downloading information from the Internet, or visiting a specialty store to add more items to his growing collection.

Batter Up
Make two teams by finding another family of three, four, or more. Play ball.

Special Events

Plan a unique outing that's not necessarily costly and schedule it monthly or bimonthly so everyone can look forward to it. Talk about it off and on to build up anticipation. Possibilities include kayaking, boating, cross-country skiing, or attending children's theater or puppet shows.

Space Permitting

Set up a volleyball net or croquet set in your yard.

We Were There

Take a short trip. Send your child a postcard from places you visited together even for the day or a few hours. Write, "We had a great time, didn't we?" or, "Loved being with you."

After the Fact

Whatever you do, relive the experiences to ingrain them in your child's mind. Discuss the event, its "wrong turns," coincidences, and happy or humorous happenings.

Special Circumstances

When *You* Travel

You can pursue "little things" even when you are away on business or vacation and your children are at home. The more of these suggestions you implement, the less likely they will miss you too much. These ideas can also help reduce your anxiety about the kids' happiness and minimize any guilt you may feel about being away.

Continue Chit-Chats
When you call home to say goodnight, announce "chit-chat" time and discuss what you would if you were home putting your child to bed.

I See You
Use your cellphone or other device to take pictures of yourself at the airport, at your destination, at local sites or in your hotel room. Send them to the kids to reassure them that you are fine.

Wish I Could be There

Ask a friend, another parent, or an older child to take a video of your child's sporting event, recital, or special activity that you will miss. Once at home, enjoy viewing it *with* your child.

Story Time, Long Distance

Download a copy of the book you are reading together to keep nightly reading uninterrupted via the phone.

Take Good Care

While you are out of town lend your child something—a pen, a hat, gloves, or your favorite mug or cup—that you use frequently but will not need while you are gone.

Supremely Organized

You may feel better (read: less guilty) if you arrange your young child's outfits for the days you will be away. What your child wore that day can fill in the conversation gaps when you call home.

Not Out of Sight

Leave a photograph of yourself in the kid's room or on the refrigerator door.

Special Circumstances

Missing You
Tell your children when you miss them and remind them that you will be home soon. Count the days together when you call or have them cross days off on a calendar. Add a big smile or heart in the day you plan to return.

Big Bed
Every now and then while you are away, allow your child to sleep in your bed as an extra privilege.

Soft and Fluffy
Give your child your pillow to sleep with whenever you travel.

Oversized
One of Dad's or Mom's t-shirts is the perfect child's nightshirt when you are not home.

Nightly Sighting
Connect electronically via face-to-face video program to allow your children to see and chat with you daily.

The Unexpected
Leave short notes in surprising places for your child to discover.

Go Easy

Ease off on some of your normal rules and routines when you're traveling—allow your child to stay up a few extra minutes before bedtime, to watch an extra television program, or to have a favorite meal twice.

E-Greeting

Send an animated or musical e-card to remind your children that you may be away, but they are in your thoughts.

Friends Help

Schedule more playtime with friends or ask if a friend can stay one night for an early dinner with your child, even though it's a school night.

Prized Possession

The free pad of paper, pen, or shampoo in your hotel room that is meaningless to you can be a young child's prized possession. Bring them home.

City by City

Instead of purchasing useless junk, buy a mug with a city logo or sports team emblem from each city you visit on business. Mugs get used for years by the recipient or the entire family. Caps and city or state spoons make interesting collections.

Special Circumstances

Today was Rainy
Mail postcards home every day or two. Explain something about the city, a special building, historical sight or unusual meal to help your children feel a part of your trip.

Welcome Home
Plan a simple welcome home celebration in honor of your return: a favorite meal, treat, or activity.

You and Me
Reconnect with each child separately with time alone with you before or after you do something special with the whole family.

Flight #1272
Have your spouse and children meet you for the weekend at the end of a business trip. Look online for low weekend rates and special weekend family packages.

Business Pal

Bring your kids to conventions whenever possible.
Business trips with lengthy flights and long, lonely
evenings are opportunities to spend extended time
with your children. During the day many hotels offer
childcare and supervised activities.

Room Service

It's cozy and children adore it. Once you have
decided, allow your child to place the order.

Special Circumstances

Sick Days

The kindnesses a parent displays for a child who is ill are all expressions of love. Being apart from your child when she is not feeling well is a fact of life for many parents, so try not to feel guilty. Whether or not you are there every minute, warm memories blossom from your "royal" treatment and thoughtfulness as you help your child recover.

Long Stem
Bring home a single rose or pick a small bunch of flowers for the patient's room.

Believing
Acknowledge that your child doesn't feel well if he says so. Ask what is wrong and offer suggestions that may make him feel better.

Don't Panic
Do not overreact or continue asking the patient how she feels. By staying calm you let your child know that you are in control and that she can feel safe in your care.

What Service!
As a special treat, bring your patient his food in bed, even if he is well enough to come to the table.

Fancy, Fancy
An attractive tray makes the food more appetizing. Use a bright-colored napkin, dishes you don't use everyday, and Dad's or Mom's coffee mug for soup.

It's All in the Preparation
Prepare foods differently for the bedridden (or couch-ridden) patient: cut toast into triangles or small squares, make a milkshake and serve in a fancy glass, and include a straw with sodas and juices.

Nurse Jones
Refer to yourself as the nurse and take your child's temperature or dispense medicine with hospital-like fanfare. Do it with a sense of humor.

Special Circumstances

Explanations Help
Be sure your child understands the process of regaining her health. For example, explain how the medicine works or why she needs liquids to aid the body's healing. Explain as best you can what will happen during a doctor's visit or hospital stay.

Choices
The ill child will feel more in control if allowed to decide between two juices or two foods. Give choices whenever possible: a bath or a sponge bath, a game of Sorry or of Clue.

Couch Potato
Let your patient spend the day on the couch or in your bed.

Tender, Loving Care
Wash the patient, give her clean pajamas, comb her hair (into a new style if she's up to it), and puff the pillows before returning her to bed.

Calling All Parents
Instead of having to yell for your attention, your child should have a bell to ring.

At His Fingertips

Set up a table or use an existing nightstand to have everything the patient needs within easy reach—including water, tissues, crayons, and books.

It's Lunchtime

If you work nearby, stop home during your lunch break to say hello or to share a meal with your homebound child.

A Fresh Look

Brighten up the sickroom with blankets, sheets, and pillowcases your child does not normally use.

Be Patient

Don't send your child back to school before he is ready.

How are You Feeling?

Call home from the office several times a day to check on your sick child, to speak with her, and to reassure yourself.

Early Arrival

The day is long for a sick child. Come home as early as possible to be with him.

Special Circumstances

Extra Attention
When you are home during a child's recuperation, check on her frequently with lots of extra kisses and hugs.

Magic Hour
Give your child something to look forward to. Set a specific hour—late afternoon, or before or after dinner—when you will play a game with her or read a book.

In Reserve
Keep a few brand new activity books stashed away to give to a sick child before you go to work.

Bedtime Busywork
Promise to bring home a surprise and do so—whether a coloring book, a new set of markers or crayons, a puzzle book, a reading book, or a model kit.

Bedridden and Bored
Break up the monotony of being sick with a hat and card trick. Place the hat on the end of the bed and have your child see how many cards she can toss into it.

I Need You

Be sure the sick child knows that he can call you during the night and that you will be there if he needs you.

On the Mend

Put Mom's favorite bubble bath in the water.

Another's Illness

When a child learns of a friend's injury or illness, take the time to explain and to answer his questions. Invariably, young children worry that the same fate will befall them.

Special Days

HAPPY HOLIDAYS

Whatever and however you celebrate your holidays, it is important to include rituals and family traditions. Making your children part of happy celebrations fuels feelings of closeness for all family members. The holidays—whether Presidents' Day, Halloween, or Christmas—offer fertile ground for creating positive family togetherness. Repetition is fundamental to building tradition and holidays provide the perfect excuse to do so.

Helping prepare for a holiday is central to any festivity and gives your children the opportunity to show off. Ask the kids to draw pictures to hang, to make name tags or place cards (even if everyone knows each other), to mix ingredients, or perhaps to make a decoration for the front door. Reuse some of their works of art for the next time the holiday rolls around. Pay attention to the activities that especially capture your children's attention and turn them into annual events.

Little Holidays, Big Deal

Make a big deal out of the small holidays. Drop green food coloring into a batch of cookie dough on St. Patrick's Day, bring home a cherry pie for Presidents' Day, or buy candied apples for Halloween.

Instant Holiday

Turn a holiday meal into a celebration by purchasing theme-decorated paper napkins and plates—with shamrocks for St. Patrick's Day, hearts for Valentine's Day, flags for July 4th, pumpkins for Halloween, bunnies for Easter, and flowers for Mother's Day. Save any decorations you buy for next year.

Fat Tuesday

Pancakes for dinner. On the eve of Mardi Gras— the last night before Lent—make a pancake dinner (the traditional purpose was to use up all the fat in the house).

Toasted

Have the kids select their own pumpkin from a farm or a farmer's market. Before it gets a Halloween face, separate the seeds from the innards of the pumpkin to cook and salt or season with your children's favorite spices. Pumpkin seeds are much more fun to eat when you have prepared them at home in a skillet, oven, or microwave. Check online for cooking directions.

Special Days

Happy, Sad, or Scary

Set aside a half an hour after dinner to carve or paint faces on one large family pumpkin or on smaller ones for each child to call one his own.

Memorable Creatures

It often takes less time to pull a homemade costume together than it does to go to the store to buy one. For sure, the pillowcase that turns your child into a ghost, the yarn tail you sew on pink tights to start a bunny outfit, or the plaid shirt and straw hat that transform your boy or girl into a scarecrow makes a much longer lasting impression than a costume taken out of a box. Perhaps it's because a parent made it.

Transformation

Turn your yard into a graveyard or Halloween haven with whatever decoration you or your children choose. Pack it up and set it out each year. You can find lots of decoration ideas online.

History Lesson

How did Halloween get started? Explain the history and meaning of this holiday. Search: "History of Halloween."

Trick or Treat
Keep your child company (and safe) as she goes from door to door.

In Costume
Your child will know you are in the spirit of the holiday if you don a mask, a baseball cap, a complete costume, or a strange combination of clothing just to answer the doorbell.

Looking Over the Loot
Have your child pour his treats out on the table for you to make a safety check. You might select and ask for several pieces of your favorite candy while you're at it. The kids will remember that Mom took all the licorice and Dad wanted the Snickers bars.

Too Scary, Not Scary Enough
Rent an age-appropriate Halloween movie and cuddle up on the couch a few days before or on the day of Halloween.

Long-Lasting Holiday
Store extra Halloween candy in a container in the freezer to pack in lunches or for snacks and to slow down the post-trick-or-treat frenzy.

Special Days

Be Mine
Remember your child on Valentine's Day with a card and a note that explains something you appreciate about her helpfulness or personality.

No Card, No Gift
Simply ask your child if he or she will be your Valentine. Let your child know in words that you are so happy he is in your life.

Valentine Assistant
Ask your children's opinion on what to give your partner and then have them help you wrap—or make—the special surprise you decide on.

What to Wear?
Something red, of course! Tie a red ribbon in your or your daughter's hair.

Kisses, Kisses Everywhere
Leave a trail of chocolate kisses leading to a present or maybe just to nowhere.

You've Got Heart(s)
Cut out paper hearts to place under your children's favorite muffins, cereal bowls, or milk glasses. Spread small red paper hearts around the table like confetti.

Spread the Word

Scatter heart-shaped candies with messages on them to decorate the dinner table. Take turns reading them every year.

All Heart

Buy heart-shaped baking pans to make an annual Valentine's Day cake. Ask your child to help. Bake a strawberry pie or strawberry shortcake, serve crushed strawberries or raspberries over ice cream. Shortcut: Stop at the bakery for a cake or cupcakes with pink icing or red sprinkles.

Valentine Lunch

Cut bread into hearts to make a Valentine sandwich for the kids' lunches.

The Color Red

Red says "I Love You" on Valentine's Day. Use a red table cloth or simply put some red roses on the table.

Pets Included

Give the dog or cat a special treat too. Have your child add a red bow to your pet's collar or leash.

Special Days

Say Cheese

Every Mother's and/or Father's Day, have someone snap the family photo. Save the best shot from each year. As they accumulate, put four or five of them together in an album or frame. It's a happy record of the passing years.

Major Fun, Major Mess

Starting close, have two children toss a raw egg back and forth. Increase the distance after each successful catch. Of course this Easter event is an outdoor only one.

Egg Hunt I

Local hotels and inns often plan Easter egg hunts. Join in, then stay for brunch.

Egg Hunt II

Make the hunt a neighborhood happening with each family contributing a predetermined number of decorated eggs.

Easy Find

Instead of leaving the Easter basket in plain sight, hide it. Say "warmer" or "colder" as your children get closer or farther away from the hiding spots.

A Tisket, a Tasket

Dress up the same basket. Change its look each year by changing the color ribbons, straw, and treats you put in it.

The Healthy Basket

It is possible to fill baskets with healthy snacks and colorful eggs to make a nutritious Easter.

Happy Birthday, America

Take the children to the local parade or fireworks display every July 4th.

The Red, White, and Blue

To recognize Independence Day, hang the flag in front of your house or put small ones out for each child.

The Winner is ...

Hand out red, white, and blue crepe paper and streamers to neighborhood children for a bicycle-decorating contest. Every year hold a bicycle parade with parents or visiting guests as "judges."

Special Days

Back-to-School Celebration
A backyard family party clearly marks the end of summer and the start of the school year. Serve your children's favorite summer foods as you spend the last moments of summer together.

Sprinkles, Flour, Brown Sugar
Have your children help unpack the groceries for all holiday preparations. Just seeing sprinkles to decorate cookies or the bags of flour and sugar to make them will put the whole family in the holiday mood.

Weighing In
To insure children help with the baking, ask them which cookies they would like to make...or help you make.

Holiday Staple
Include at least one preferred dish or dessert at every holiday meal. This might be an unusual stuffing for the turkey, sweet potatoes with marshmallows, or a chocolate pie that your great-grandmother made.

Be Adventuresome
Try a new recipe that might fast become your family's first choice.

On Display

Whatever decorating you do for the holidays—skeleton cutouts on the front door, setting up the train set, or putting out a certain bowl to hold greeting cards—use them annually. The decoration or its holder will become special to your children over the years. They will look for these touches as significant parts of their holiday.

The Good Old Days

Family gatherings are ideal for videotaping elder family members. Ask each of them to relate a family tale or something from childhood. These videos at holiday celebrations will eventually grow to be a highly personal family history your children will treasure.

Wishing

Save and dry the wishbone from holiday turkeys or chickens for the children to break a few days later. When the "leftovers" are long gone, the wishbone extends festive spirit a bit longer.

Special Days

Gobble, Gobble
Heighten Thanksgiving delight by putting a small chocolate turkey at each child's place setting.

Pumpkin Pie? Yuck!
Traditional Thanksgiving pies may not appeal to your young set. Augment the dessert offerings with sweets more suited to their taste: a seven-layer cake, brownies, or cupcakes.

Cooking Specialist
Have one child become the stuffing mixer, and another be the potato masher, pie dough roller, or ingredient measurer. Children quickly assume ownership of a dish and will proudly announce, "I made that."

All Together Now
Unless the children make a special request, don't isolate them at a separate table in another room. Rent or borrow a larger table, or purchase a large collapsible one you can store in the closet so that everyone can enjoy the holiday meal together.

Don't Put Aunt Lynda Next to Uncle Gordon

Let the children arrange the seating for holiday dinners and mix it up a bit if they wish. For festive place cards, use plain white ones and have the kids draw a turkey or add an appropriate sticker. Since many of the same people attend holiday meals, save the place cards for next year. Allow the children to decide next year if they would like to improve on their artwork by making new ones.

Thanksgiving Turkey Trot

Join a community organized walk or run or start your own turkey trot with family, friends, and neighbors. Keep the distance realistic for your youngest and oldest walkers and runners. If you are feeling ambitious, make a few ribbon awards to hand out to all who cross the "finish line."

Spilling Allowed

Eliminate holiday intimidation and endear yourself to the youngest guests by making a formal announcement not to worry about spills or dropped food. Save your best tablecloths for formal dining, not for holiday meals with children.

Special Days

Walk it Off

"Walk it off" is a fun tradition for adults and children and a welcomed pause after the main course to make room for dessert. Go outside and take a walk for 15 or 20 minutes. Supervise young children who prefer to play outside.

The Menorah, the Tree

Take the whole family shopping to pick out special holiday items and decorations such as a new Menorah for Chanukah or a Christmas tree.

Recorded Rituals

Video your holiday rituals—trimming the tree, lighting the candles, or singing holiday songs—each year. It will become your family's record of good times with relatives.

Chose it Myself

Take each child shopping individually for gifts he wants to give to those people on his holiday list.

Gently Used Gifts

Bring the children along to check out garage sales and flea markets for great buys. You will all find treasures, including items you hadn't thought of, to delight the youngest—and oldest—family members.

A Caring Tradition

At holiday time, have everyone in the family search through closets and chests for coats, clothing, and toys to donate. Also have the kids help you decide what canned foods on your shelf to give to a shelter or food bank.

Wrap it Up

Whatever the holiday or celebration, have children who are old enough help gift-wrap the presents. To speed things along and make it more fun, set up a "wrapping station" on a table with paper, kid-safe scissors, tape, ribbons, crayons, markers, and stickers from which children can pick what they like.

Tagged

An especially delightful approach for to/from name tags for presents is to use prints of photos of the giver and recipient. Photos taken when the children were very young are the most fun.

Holiday Delivery

Take your children on a meaningful errand to select, buy and deliver gifts for children in the hospital, a homeless shelter or to another social service group .

Special Days

T'is the Week Before ...

... and excitement levels are soaring. Children need more parental time, direction, and structure to keep them calm and occupied. Try to get home earlier from work and plan to accomplish some of the holiday busywork with your children.

Holiday Bake-In

Far in advance of the big day, while you are still feeling relaxed, select cookie recipes and make cookies that children can decorate. Bake and store in your freezer.

"A" is for Andrew

Use the tail end of the cookie batter to shape your child's initial into a cookie he decorates.

Gingerbread House

Bake and decorate gingerbread houses together. This is an impressive and splendid labor of love that's worth the time in the memory department. Kits are available for this particular enterprise and make it much easier for all.

Extra Kisses

Hang mistletoe in heavily trafficked areas of the house: over the refrigerator door, by the back door, outside the bathroom, or by your child's bedroom door (when you wake her up or tuck her in, it's an automatic extra kiss).

Time Out

Find five minutes in each hectic holiday to have private time with each child to listen, relax, or just sit close by.

Town Tour

Drive or walk around the neighborhood one evening to see the homes and streets decorated with holiday lights.

Frosty

Be willing to get cold and wet building a snowman, sledding, or ice skating with the kids.

Come In from the Cold

Keep marshmallows and ingredients on hand to make hot chocolate after wintery outdoor activities.

Tree Traditions

Go into the woods and cut down your Christmas tree every year. If you purchase "balled" trees, you can plant them after the holiday and watch them grow for years to come.

The Angel Goes on the Top

Choose tree-decorating time carefully—when children are rested and adults are not preoccupied. Plan it as a family event.

What the Tree Needs

Handmade ornaments are quick and easy to knit or needlepoint. Add a new one each year. You can find appropriate patterns online or at a local craft shop that children can make. Help your child make an ornament with his photograph and the date.

This is My Favorite

As you decorate, reminisce with the kids about the ornaments—tell where they came from, who made them, and any unique stories behind them. Use and save all ornaments your children make.

For Grandma and Grandpa

With your children's help, honoring their preferences, comb through your digital photos to pull together shots of your children at different ages and turn them into a gift calendar for the upcoming year for their grandparents. It's a gift that all involved will love.

The Stockings Were Hung

Your children's stockings are for a lifetime. Whether you buy, knit, needlepoint, or have someone else make them, the stockings you have are a very special part of Christmas. Be sure they are of good quality so they have staying power.

Dear Santa

On Christmas Eve, have the kids leave a note to Santa with some cookies and milk—perhaps a few carrots for the reindeer. It's an old ritual, but one kids continue to love. You might even leave a Santa response to be discovered in the morning.

Young Santas

To help instill the spirit of giving, have the children pass out the presents one at a time. Wait until the person has opened the gift to move on.

Special Days

I Can't Wait

If your tradition is to open all gifts on Christmas morning, allow the kids to open one gift on Christmas Eve; if your tradition is to open all gifts on Christmas Eve, save one present per person for Christmas morning.

Where is It?

Hide one gift for each child to find.

Stocking Grab Bag Style

Find a large Christmas stocking or decorative bag, create your own, and fill it with balls, ornaments, jacks, crayons, and small items you know your children would like. After each child pulls out his "prize," allow all of them to trade if they wish.

The High Sign

Agree on a signal your kids can use to alert you when they want to talk to you alone, away from the commotion and excitement.

A Family Tale

Write a fun or fantasy short story about your family— its members near and far, its achievements, and its goals—to read as part of one evening's festivities.

Strawberry Pancakes

Establish a traditional holiday morning breakfast in your house—a special kind of pancakes, coffee cake, sticky buns, omelets, or jelly-filled crepes, a dish you know your family prefers.

Windows

Avoid the crowds viewing the store windows in your city's shopping area by going the day after Christmas. After all, Christmas is a season, not a day. Stop for hot chocolate.

The Nutcracker

Attend high school holiday plays, which are almost always appropriate for young children. Save the longer, professional productions for when the children are older.

Dress Up

Put on festive clothing for holiday dinners, outings, and get-togethers.

Tradition

Serve one or more traditional dishes during Chanukah.

Special Days

Light the Lights
Use the same Menorah each year.

First or Last
Be consistent about handing out Chanukah gifts.
Determine whether that time will be before or after
lighting the candles or at the conclusion of dinner.

Toast Master
Allow each child to make a toast or offer thanks for a
holiday meal. If you pray before the meal, let the kids
take turns from year to year in leading the prayer.

Salute
Reserve extra minutes before you go off to your
own party to deliver Happy New Year cheer to your
children. Serve a special snack and soft drinks in fancy
glasses for toasting. Leave the kids party hats and
noisemakers and call home just before their bedtime.

At-Home New Year's Eve
Make your New Year's Eve menu as traditional as the
one you set for Thanksgiving so that the family will
have another festivity to look forward to.

A Few of My Favorite Things

When the family is gathered for a family New Year's celebration or the children's dinner before you go out, talk about everyone's favorite thing about the year that is ending.

A Family New Year's Resolution

Make a joint resolution that includes everyone in the family: to hug hello and goodbye, to let a person finish what he is saying without interrupting, to honor each person's personal space, or to not borrow something without asking.

Waiting for Midnight

Reserve one game from the children's gift pile with the express intent of playing it as part of a family New Year's Eve celebration.

Greenwich Mean Time

For young children, use Greenwich Mean Time for the New Year's celebration. They can wear their celebration hats, shout out "Happy New Year," and blast their noisemakers. Greenwich Mean Time is much earlier than every time zone in the U.S. and a GMT celebration time means all the kids will have a longer night's sleep.

Special Days

Memorable Birthdays

Birthdays, like holidays, are naturals for instilling tradition. Your children's birthdays commemorate that they are part of your life. They are days to recognize and honor how important and special each of your children is. In addition to the ones here, you may come up with your own unique ways to celebrate. Be sure to repeat the birthday rituals you start every year.

Birthday Wake-Up
Tie a balloon around the juice glass, and put a birthday napkin next to the birthday child's cereal bowl.

Queen/King for a Day
Make or purchase a crown or unique birthday hat that the celebrant wears each year at her party or, for that matter, all day if she wishes.

It's Your Birthday

Include your child in the party planning. Ask for her cake preference, if she wants special activities and games, and of course what friends she wants to invite (while keeping the number manageable). Being part of the planning process enriches her day even more.

Purple Icing

Siblings appreciate being included in the birthday child's big day. Have the kids help out in making or decorating the cake. Be ready for bright or strange-colored icing. It will be remembered.

Designer Cakes

On the other hand, if you're the cake chef with a special talent for unusual or highly original cakes, photograph your effort to preserve the memory of your creativity and hard work in your child's mind. You can find lots of shape and theme suggestions and cake-decorating ideas online.

My Choice is ...

Birthday cake can be a pie. If that is what the birthday child likes best, why not?

Special Days

Early Risers
Leave a gift on the end of your child's bed so he wakes up to a present.

All Day Surprises
Scatter gifts throughout the day—put one in her backpack, one in the lunch box, and one on the kitchen table as a birthday welcome home from school.

Hidden Treasures
Hide gifts in one or two rooms around the house.

Flying Balloons
Hang a balloon from the mailbox, a tree, or the doorknob to welcome the birthday child home from school. It can turn into a wonderful tradition.

How Pretty
Decorate simply. Some balloons, a few colorful streamers, and birthday napkins are enough to fill the bill.

Traditional Signs
Buy or design a "Happy Birthday" banner to hang year after year.

Honoring Requests

Give in to silly birthday requests … and make them a standing part of your child's birthday for years to come. If your three- or five-year-old wants her name spelled out in Cheerios on her birthday cake, she will get a kick out of it even when she's 15.

A Private Affair

Reserve one evening for celebrating the birth of your child by having dinner with just your partner and child or children—no extended family members or friends—to recognize and honor how important your family unit is.

Place of Honor

Seat the celebrant at the head of the dinner table.

Interesting Invitations

Turn your young child's drawing into a party invitation. Write the party information below the picture or on the other side and make as many copies as you need.

Special Days

Do-It-Yourself Cloth

Spread a plain (heavyweight) white paper cloth or put large sheets of drawing paper at each place setting with an individual box or group of crayons. Ask each guest to decorate his or her own place at the party table.

Double Dare

The theme is the thing—from a double dare obstacle course to Treasure Island hunts with a search for the prize. Use a different theme each year: learn how to hula-hoop at a Hawaiian theme party, and then create an obstacle course of tires to jump through for a Double Dare party.

Blindfolded and Swinging

Hang a piñata. No need to be fancy; use a paper bag filled with candy or small toys. Careful supervision is required when the swinging starts to make sure only the piñata gets hit.

Memorable Memorabilia

Save birthday cards, unusual bows, and cake or room decorations. Also stow away a copy of the party invitation, a birthday napkin, and a group photo of the guests from each party.

Private Birthday

Select a day close to your child's birthday for a private celebration—just the two of you. It's the birthday child's chance to plan the day: a train ride, a boat ride, a trip to a special store, or a picnic in the park or at the zoo. It can be that simple for younger children.

The Art of Giving

Take your child shopping for birthday gifts for other members of the family … and for her friends.

Record the Year

Write a short letter to your children each year on their birthdays. For younger children, record milestones and progress; for older children, mention accomplishments or include family highlights of the year.

One to Grow With

Plant a birthday tree or shrub in the yard and watch it flourish with your child. Oak, pine, maple, and cedar trees grow quickly, so you will be able to note progress from year to year. Name a planting for each child: Tammy's Tree, Ted's Bush, and Christopher's Ivy. When it needs water or plant food, ask your child to help nourish his or her birthday planting.

Little Things Long Remembered

Childhood is an adventure, a journey to be joined by parents whenever possible. Slow down so you can grab pockets of time together—even a few minutes here and there. In these short intervals you give a child a clear sense of security and attachment to you, to your family unit, and to your larger family.

The "little things long remembered" in this section help develop the sense of belonging and build an environment in which your child will feel loved and appreciated. At the same time you will be creating and preserving your child's childhood with sweet remembrances and strengthening your bond.

Step off your hectic treadmill frequently in order to pack in as many "little things" as you can to create lasting memories. Minimum effort—and sometimes no effort at all because some memories create themselves—brings maximum results in the memory department. Your child will look back and say, "I had such a happy childhood." And as a parent, you will say, "I did my job well."

Don't Leave it Behind

Take the identification tag from your baby's hospital bassinet and save it or place it at the beginning of his first photo album. If you store photos electronically, scan the tag into your computer.

Famous Firsts

Be on hand for every first you can: first bus ride, first train ride, first trip to the dentist, first day of school, first friend's birthday party, and first movie in a theater.

Cheering Section

Celebrate individual triumphs as a family. Bravos for children's accomplishments can include serving the particular child's desired menu. A rousing round of applause from everyone at the table encourages the child who struggles as well as the child who achieves and masters challenges with ease.

Gather 'Round

Celebrate with as many relatives as possible for as many of the holidays as you can. Years from now, when your children look back at holidays, they will think of family and good times.

Little Things Long Remembered

For Posterity

Document significant family happenings or school functions with photographs or video—from first words and steps to graduating to a two-wheeler bicycle, from first Little League games to birthday celebrations. Remember to do this for all your children—not just your firstborn.

Questions with Answers

Do you know what Aunt Rachael did before she became a mom? Do you know what she does now? Did you know that Grandpa Jake made men's suits and then decided to be a lawyer? Include both failures and successes in the stories about the extended family members. This will give your children the awareness that theirs is a family that can bounce back when down and celebrate when life goes well.

Please, Come with Us

Make or find the time to escort your child on a class trip. Your presence will be a lasting recollection.

What We Did Last Summer

Prepare a photo album or a computer generated display of your family's summer activities. Next spring go through it with the kids to ask what they would like to repeat.

Getting to Know Me

Introduce your child to your place of employment by arranging a short visit when the office is in operation. If you work in a facility that children aren't allowed to visit, ask a co-worker to take photographs of you "in action."

Office Outing

If possible, suggest an office picnic or special outing that includes children so yours can meet your colleagues.

Remembrances of Things Past

Take pictures of your child's bedroom every few years so she will be able to recall it as it was. Also photograph the exterior of your home and your child's school.

Packing Up and Moving On

If or when you relocate, plan a party before you move for your children and their friends. Take lots of pictures and turn them into an online photo album your children will cherish.

Little Things Long Remembered

One for the Book!

Keep a simple computer log of each child's milestones, funny comments, adventures, and triumphs. These will become important documentation of time spent together and will be revisited often as your children grow. Tell older children when something they did is going "in the book."

Talent Show

Hold a semi-annual talent show at home for your children and their friends. Fun abounds even if what you hear are unrecognizable tunes, though played and sung enthusiastically and loudly.

Break Your Own Rules

On occasion, announce "Rule Break" and make an exception to a standing rule: "Rule Break: Tonight you can sleep on the couch," or, "Rule Break: I will walk the dog so you can watch TV."

Just Moved

Acquaint yourself and your kids with your new neighborhood. Make it an exciting expedition to find stores, parks, school, restaurants, and the police and fire stations in your new locale.

New Home

Have a celebration on the first night in a new house or apartment. Toast with soda or milk and cookies and make a big bowl of popcorn for everyone to munch on while you unpack.

Fantasy

For car trips, waiting rooms, or when there is nothing to do, make up stories about people you don't really know. The policeman you just passed lives in a huge castle; the nurse in the doctor's office is a ballet dancer at night. Ask your child to develop the stories.

Buffet Night

Turn dinner into an occasional buffet. Put out whatever leftovers you have along with sandwich and salad fixings. The diners get to put whatever they want on their plates.

And the Band Played On

Got rhythm? A touch of talent? You don't really need either to form a family band. The youngest can play drums on a pot with chopsticks or spoons, your aspiring violinist, guitarist, or piano player can play along, and everyone can sing. The sounds that emerge will be memorable … and chances are good that they will improve as the family band gains experience.

Charity Choices

The family's chosen charities are likely to remain your child's preferred charities into his or her adulthood. Discuss several causes you feel are worthwhile and have your child help you decide the ones to support. Older children generally have charity group ideas of their own. Ask them to explain why their favorites deserve your support.

It Adds Up

Keep a container for your loose coins and periodically count it with your child. When there's enough, give the money to a charity your family likes to support or to the victims of a recent tragedy.

Watch Money Grow

Go to the bank together to open a savings account in your child's name.

Community Service

Explore community service organizations in your area to find out how you and your children might be of assistance. Are there food banks or soup kitchens nearby that need help? Do they allow children to participate? Help out wherever and as often as you can as a family.

The Envelope, Please

Instead of just handing over gift money, a check, or allowance, put it in small, colored envelopes. Always use the same color, and the envelope will quickly become an unusual family custom your children will remember gleefully.

My Stuff

Purchase a bath towel, a rocking chair, a mug, or a cereal bowl—any item that is frequently in use—with your child's name on it.

Save Box

Be sure to pack away your children's favorite books, stuffed animals, and other memorabilia, such as a well-worn play kitchen or train set. The Save Box not only triggers memories, but also allows them to share their childhood with their own children.

Dream House

Over time—possibly years—decorate a dollhouse with your child.

Workin' on the Railroad

Start with a little bit of track and a few railroad cars and build it into a major railroad by adding more cars, track, and station houses over the next decade or two.

Little Things Long Remembered

Do Not Open Until ...
In a separate, plastic, waterproof box or similar container, label it, "History for the Future." Add a few magazines or newspaper coverage of important events, a list of books you and your children are reading, what movies are popular, and a stack or CD of family and friends' photos that reflect what is happening that year. Seal it up and mark, "Do Not Open Until (insert a year 20 or so years from now)." Tuck your time capsule away for safe-keeping.

The Past in Song
Sing songs popular when you were growing up. The children may think your "performance" is perfectly awful. They'll complain, but will eventually remember your singing with affection.

Happy Un-Birthday to You
Chose a day roughly six months from a child's real birthday and deem it her un-birthday. Give it a silly name and let her choose what she would like to wear, to do, and to eat on her half-birthday.

Swinging
Hang a tire swing in the backyard. Raise it higher as your child grows.

Tall Tales

Save your family's made-up stories—especially ones in which the children are the main characters—for them to reread.

T-Shirt Quilt

Store your child's outgrown souvenir t-shirts—those collected from vacations, received as gifts, or brought home from your business trips—to turn into a quilt. You may need to turn the job over to someone else, or do it yourself in your retirement years.

Do Over

When you find a vacation or camping spot the whole family enjoys, return on a regular basis so that it becomes a tradition.

Voting Power

Plan vacations as a family. As children get older, give them more say in where you go.

No Extra Vacation Days

Can't get enough time off? Send your child to visit or on a trip with a grandparent or aunt, uncle, or cousins.

Little Things Long Remembered

Awards Ceremony
At the last dinner or lunch of a family vacation, present awards to each of the children. Awards need not be fancy: a tennis ball to the most enthusiastic sports person, a used paperback to the one who read the most, candy to the most congenial, or a comic book to the funniest. Make up awards to fit the activities you engaged in.

Picture This
Ask your son or daughter to organize your digital or scanned photographs to create a family album around a single family event. Give credit for its creation whenever you show it.

Cuddle Up
It may take you some time, but knit or crochet a scarf, a sweater, or if feeling very ambitious, an afghan. One homemade item—even mittens or a hat—makes a lasting, loving impression on a child.

Pen Pal
Do an Internet search for "pen pals for kids." It will come up with names from many countries such as Sweden, Greece, Andorra, Japan, and the Ivory Coast. Help your child keep the correspondence going. Maybe one day she will end up visiting her pen pal.

Property of Ryan Jones
Order inexpensive pencils and stationery online imprinted with your child's name.

Back to Nature
Try to keep the creatures your child finds outside—box turtles, lizards, and crickets—long enough to emblazon their discovery in his mind before releasing them back to their natural environment.

Naming Names
Get the whole family involved in deciding on what to call a new pet. Vote on proposed names if everyone can't agree or put them in a hat and draw the winning name.

In the Mail or Online
Order subscriptions to magazines that interest your child at different stages and through different phases.

On My Own
The first few times your child goes away with another family or to spend time with relatives, slip a note into her suitcase as a reminder that you love her and are thinking about her.

Little Things Long Remembered

On Arrival
Mail a letter or postcard ahead so it's waiting for your child when she arrives for her first day of camp each year.

Surprise Packages
Every now and then, instead of carrying in shopping bags, have the store ship the purchases you made for your children directly to them.

Keepsakes
Find a sturdy box, a plastic or metal storage container, or a durable folder to store programs, buttons, ticket stubs, and other "treasures" from events your child attends.

Capture an Age
Consider having an artist paint an oil or watercolor portrait of your child or blow up, print, and frame a fabulous photo.

We Want a Dog
Bring home a turtle or a few goldfish.

Little Things Long Remembered
Bring home a kitten or a puppy.

Susan Newman, PhD, is a social psychologist focusing on issues related to raising children and family relationships. She is the author of 15 books and blogs about parenting for *Psychology Today* magazine.

Dr. Newman is a member of the American Psychological Association, the Authors Guild, and the American Society of Journalists and Authors and is a Court-Appointed Special Advocate (CASA) for abused and neglected children.

She lives in the New York Metro area and is the mother of one son and four stepchildren. Visit her website at www.susannewmanphd.com.

CPSIA information can be obtained
at www.ICGtesting.com
Printed in the USA
BVHW060154210620
581896BV00002B/24

9 780991 466009